Stuck in a Funk?

How to Get Your Church Moving Forward

Tony Morgan

The contents of this book were previously published as individual eBooks in the Leisure Suit series:

- *The Leisure Suit Trap: 8 Reasons Your Church Is Stuck*
- *Hanging Up the Leisure Suit: How to Get Unstuck*
- *Stayin' Alive: Build a Legacy of Leadership*
- *Get Your Groove On: 12 Ideas to Help You Communicate Through Change*

I believe you have to be willing to be misunderstood if you're going to innovate . . . That's actually a serious point. If you're going to do something that's never been done before—which is basically what innovation is—people are going to misunderstand it just because it's new.

—Jeff Bezos, Amazon.com founder & CEO

Contents

Part Four: Get Your Groove On
Communicate Through Change 75

Introduction

When I work with churches for the first time, I think sometimes their leaders are frustrated with me because I'm not willing to help them fix something specific. Sometimes they want me to tweak their internal systems. Other times they want me to speak into improvements in their Sunday service environments. Other times they want me to provide feedback on their Web site, music, or facility. I've found that churches can become convinced that they know why their church isn't growing.

There comes a point when it's healthy and appropriate to address specific environments, systems, or tactics; however, most times the reason behind a declining ministry goes much deeper. And if pastors and church leaders are unwilling to address what's at the heart of their ministry, they're going to continue seeing downward trends.

The crazy thing about this is that there are many churches more willing to close their doors than make the necessary changes it would take to have a positive effect. Why is it that we put our personal preferences ahead of our ministry impact?

The material in this book was first released as four separate eBooks that were part of the Leisure Suit series and available for download from my Web site. Through my experience working with churches across the country, as well as the many conversations I've had with pastors and church leaders and friends, I knew there was interest in how to get their churches *un*-stuck. That said, the response to the original eBooks was more than I could have ever expected.

Stuck in a Funk is broken up into four different parts:

1. **The Leisure Suit Trap** focuses on why churches are stuck, defining the challenge at hand.

2. **Hanging Up the Leisure Suit** addresses out-of-date, out-of-touch, or just plain every-day-as-normal church environments, systems, or tactics.

3. **Stayin' Alive** considers leadership changes that may be long overdue.

4. **Get Your Groove On** looks at the message you are conveying when you're not preaching—through what you say and sometimes don't say—Mondays through Saturdays.

I'm not satisfied with churches being stuck. And since you're reading this book, I know you feel the same way. It's time we set our preferences aside and prioritize making disciples of Jesus. Are you ready to hang up your "leisure suit" for good? Are you ready to get out of that funk you've been stuck in for way too long?

If you're a pastor, go through this book with your executive team or key leaders in your church. Suggest to your small group leaders and teachers that they study it together. There are questions at the back that will help you have great conversations and establish next steps. And when you've finished reading this and feel that your church is no longer stuck in a funk, please let me know about your experience.

Part One

The Leisure Suit Trap

Why Your Church Is Stuck

1

History of the Leisure Suit

My dad used to own several leisure suits. Had I been smart, I would have raided his closet and kept one of them. Since I wasn't smart enough to do that before I left home, I decided to purchase one of my own using eBay. I paid a chunk of money for it. Needless to say, Dad could have gotten rich if he would have held on to his leisure suits.

At one point the leisure suit was trendy, highly functional, everyone was wearing it, and it was easy to care for. It served a purpose: people needed to wear clothing that was functional and fashionable at the same time. What better solution than a polyester suit?

Eventually, the leisure suit went the way of the pet rock and the cassette player. They disappeared because better ideas came along. That's the way history works.

Some churches are still wearing their leisure suits. Figuratively, of course. Many churches are stuck. Though they may have had a season where their kingdom impact was expanding, things have slowed down or started to decline. They know something has to change, but many times they're unwilling to change. They'd rather keep wearing the leisure suit.

The leisure suit disappeared as fashion trends changed. Anyone caught wearing one was immediately branded as out of touch with reality or irrelevant. Sure, the leisure suit still serves a purpose, but almost no one wears them. Unfortunately, many churches still do! They sit comfortably watching the disco ball spin overhead wondering why the congregation is growing older and smaller. What they are doing is no longer connecting with today's culture. They are not seeing the fruit.

By the way, whatever you perceive to be "traditional" churches aren't the only churches that are stuck. Your church may have started one hundred years ago or ten years ago or even just ten months ago—but stuck is still *stuck*.

We can grow so accustomed to what we are doing that we are no longer aware that the rest of the world wandered off into the future. While we were counting nickels and noses, the world changed.

It's easy to strut around proclaiming, "I like my leisure suit." But does it really matter what I like? Am I here to exclaim the awesomeness of my personal preferences, or am I here to focus on those people I am called to impact? It's one or the other.

Sometimes we don't realize we aren't connected. We need fresh eyes to see that we are stuck.

What's the point? Until we look at our methods, our message really doesn't matter. When we keep trying to use the same systems—hoping and praying for different results—that's when we know we've fallen for the "leisure suit trap."

Over the last several years, I've had the opportunity to study and work with churches across the country. What follows is a list of the common attributes of churches that end up being stuck. What's your story? Are any of these attributes present in your ministry environment?

Let's unpack eight reasons why your church may be stuck.

2

You Lack a Leadership Empowerment Plan

Outreach Magazine interviewed Brad Abare and Phil Cooke about personality-driven churches. Here's a paraphrase of the list of warning signs that they identified in the interview:

- The pastor doesn't go on a vacation for any significant length of time. And, when he does, it isn't announced.
- When the pastor doesn't preach, the attendance drops.
- There's an unspoken fear that if something happened to the pastor, the church would be in trouble.
- The pastor is unwilling to listen to and consult other team members.
- The staff and volunteers are there to carry out the directions of the pastor.
- There's no succession plan in place; therefore, leadership development isn't happening.

So, what other options are there? After all, aren't we supposed to create pastoral rock stars who roam from place to place with an entourage of iPhone-toting handlers? I hate to break it to you, but . . . no. That's not the point.

Real leaders cast vision and train the next generation of leaders. Real leaders empower people to lead, refuse to step in at the last minute, and provide coaching and encouragement along the way.

I'm still a big proponent of clear vision in churches. Clear vision leads to unified effort that results in ministry impact. A clear vision also provides a lot of freedom for people to be empowered to be who God created them to be. I've heard it described as freedom within a framework. That's essentially a picture of the Christian faith. There's actually more freedom for us if we stay within God's designed framework.

We see this reflected in Paul's writings on spiritual gifts in 1 Corinthians 12 as well. Each believer is given one or more gifts. Paul uses the human body as a metaphor to express how the various parts of the body of Christ are indispensable. In other words, we have failed as leaders in the church if we do not embrace the unique gift-mix that God designed. And we won't fully know the power and impact of the local church until people are empowered to be the people God wired them up to be.

> *We aren't telling them what to do to accomplish the vision. We are helping them discover their gifts and freeing them to use them to fulfill the vision. It's not delegation. With delegation, I'm still responsible. It's empowerment. Someone else is responsible, but as a leader I still hold them accountable.*

At a recent meeting with a church staff, one of the members asked me about leadership growth. Having worked with churches of various sizes between 100 people and more than 10,000, they wanted to know how leaders change to grow with organizations. Here's what I summarized with a little bit more detail. Some of this reflects my own experiences in the churches I've served. Some of it reflects the conversations I've had with leaders in other churches.

Lead by Example. This is the type of leadership that is required when new ministries launch. During this season, leaders have to do most of the work themselves. That happens out of necessity because no one else is around. It also happens to establish a foundation for the future. "Leading by doing" gives leaders the opportunity to shape the mission, vision, values, and strategy of their churches. These folks may not necessarily be gifted as leaders, but they are in a positional leadership role. They are the "leaders of tens." Ministries with this style of leadership can grow to about one hundred people.

Lead Other People. During this season, leaders recruit other people to join their ministry team. Rather than doing all the work on their own, leaders begin to delegate tasks and responsibilities to other people. The leaders still own the responsibility for making things happen, they're just including other people in the effort. These are the "leaders of fifties." Ministries can grow to several hundred people with this style of leadership.

Lead Other Leaders. This is when a transition happens, where leaders begin to empower other leaders. Instead of a hands-on role where they're on top of all the tasks, they shift to a role where they're really more concerned about leading, caring for, and raising up other leaders. They don't give up responsibility for the outcome, but they begin to release team building, decision making, and execution to other people. These are the "leaders of hundreds." Ministries can grow to several thousand people with this style of leadership.

Lead by Vision. At some point, there are leaders who may continue to embrace functional leadership of specific areas of ministry, but their focus is really on the overall health of the church. Rather than a ministry-specific focus, they have a global perspective that encompasses every aspect of the organization. These folks are leading other leaders, but they also have influence that reaches beyond their direct reports. They are coming alongside the senior leader to champion the vision that God has given the church.

These are the "leaders of thousands." Ministries can grow to tens of thousands of people with this style of leadership.

By the way, all of these approaches to leadership are vital in a healthy, growing church. Even if I've moved to a place in my leadership where I'm primarily leading by vision, there will be instances when I need to lead by example. Where churches get stuck, though, is when only one style of leadership is evident in the top leadership team.

So, before you continue reading, do you agree with my summary of these different stages of leadership growth? What would you add or delete from my descriptions? Also, where are you? What do you need to do today to prepare to step into a new leadership role tomorrow?

3

You Are Unclear About Your Vision and Mission

A church without a clearly articulated vision is a church that's in danger. Vision is to the church what headlights are to a car in the dark. You can't go very far very safely without them.

The funny thing is there are lots of churches with vision statements, but I don't think there are very many churches that really have a vision statement that clarifies who they are as an organization. Among other things, a solid vision:

- Clarifies the purpose of the organization
- Pursues a preferred future
- Inspires people to engage
- Makes it easier to define what the organization won't do

Even with that, you may be wondering whether or not your organization has clearly defined and communicated its vision. Here are two surefire ways to know whether or not you've accomplished the goal:

A clear vision that is properly communicated will rally people. People will look at the present situation and agree together that there's a better future that must be pursued. People will give their time, energy, prayer, financial resources, talents, and gifts to help accomplish that vision. Lots of people will do that. If people aren't attracted to your church, your vision either isn't strong enough or it hasn't been communicated clearly.

A clear vision that is properly communicated will also repel people. Think of the most successful businesses or churches—Apple, Starbucks, Wal-Mart, Willow Creek, Saddleback, Billy Graham, etc. Each of these businesses or ministries has experienced huge success. If you were to Google the names of each of these organizations and the word "haters," you'll also find there are plenty of people who consider these organizations evil. Clarifying your vision will help some people determine they don't want to be a part of your cause. (And, don't be surprised if some attack.) If people aren't leaving your church, your vision either isn't strong enough or it hasn't been communicated clearly.

I want to challenge you to think about the purpose of your ministry. Does it rally people to your cause? And, does it repel some people? Of course, a healthy vision worth pursuing must attract many more people than it turns away; however, a strong vision will always help some people determine, "That's not for me."

If your sense is that you have a vision that makes everyone happy, you don't have a strong vision.

4

You Blame Outsiders and External Factors

We live in a culture where no one is responsible for anything that happens to them. If you don't believe me, invest a couple of hours watching one of the multitude of judge shows on television. (Better yet—don't do that.)

It's amazing that people instigate litigation as a result of something that happened because of a decision *they* made. On television, blaming others is entertainment. In the church, it's tragedy.

There is a tendency among church leaders to blame their ineffectiveness on the changing community, the struggling economy, or the big church that obviously watered down its message in order to reach people who are interested only in being entertained. Staff meetings must look a lot like the talks that take place every fall in the locker room of the Chicago Cubs: "This was going to be our year, but the other teams got hot, our star player got hurt, and the wind was blowing in more than out." Maybe it's time to man-up and say, "I didn't get the job done, and we've got to figure out a new approach."

I'm amazed at the "new" ideas that come from some Christian organizations that experienced their best years in the '60s and '70s. If you look closely, those new ideas look a lot like old ideas with new packaging. They are hoping to recapture their past glory by repositioning their past products. Good luck with that!

The problem, according to the organization's leaders, is the increase in competition. In other words, if people didn't have so many options, they'd be perfectly fine buying subpar products. Victims, huh?

Victim-thinking will only lead to bitterness and competition. Leaders who blame outsiders and external factors actually are confessing their own failure to think creatively and inspire their team. Churches in their leisure suits are victims of the changing taste in clothing. When the world returns to thinking the way they thought forty years ago, they'll be dressed for success. Until then, they'll look sadly out of place!

5

Your Structure Inhibits Growth

It's easy to get caught in the trap when your organizational structure and internal processes haven't evolved and are largely the same as they were three or five years ago. Or sometimes we get stuck when internal processes are too confusing to navigate, thus stifling new ideas rather than spurring innovation.

One of my favorite blogs to monitor is Accidental Creative. Todd Henry wrote a brilliant article about the danger of implementing permanent solutions to temporary problems. This quote grabbed my attention:

> *The more structures we have to navigate in order to do our work, the more difficult it is to do our best work. When we are required to resolve the dissonance of complex systems, reporting relationships, and accountability structures just in order to get our objectives and check off our direction, we will begin to lose our drive to do brilliant work. Over time, this complexity only pulls entire organizations toward systematic mediocrity.*

One of the attributes of a church in decline is a complex structure. The natural tendency of organizations is to add complexity to their structure and systems. The longer an organization exists, the more complex it typically gets.

(Think government, big business, denominations . . . and older churches.)

One of the reasons I think new church plants are so effective reaching new people is because they are typically very lean. The structure is simple. The ministry strategy is very focused. The mission is clear. Then, as the church ages, the ministry strategy gets more complex as multiple new programs and events get layered on. Eventually growth slows or plateaus as the complexity increases, and then our solution is new structure or systems or rules to fix the problem.

- If there's a problem, our natural tendency is never to do less—we always try something new.
- If there's a problem, our natural tendency is to increase controls—we think people are the problem, and we implement rules and policies to make sure they get it right.

It's quite possible the solution to the problem involves fewer controls. The fix may require less complexity.

Are you willing to get focused and lean again? Are you willing to attack complex structure and rules?

6

You Worship Your Past Success

It's easy to get caught in the trap when you stop seeing yourself as responsible or accountable for the ministry results you produce. I read a fascinating article from Forbes about how General Motors destroyed its Saturn division. Among other things, David Hanna, the author of the article, suggested:

> Saturn, a GM company that had great promise in the early 1990s, ultimately failed because senior GM leaders couldn't see the benefits of new ways of doing things and a new kind of organizational culture.

We're all familiar with the demise of GM, so this is a very vivid image of what can happen when an organization becomes so stuck in its traditional approach of doing things that the world passes it by. Ultimately, when organizations stick to "the way we do it," the safe approach of avoiding innovation and change becomes the riskiest approach.

Hanna goes on to explain:

> There were just two underlying forces behind Saturn's demise: GM's insistence on managing all its divisions centrally with a tight fist, and the demand by leadership at both GM and the UAW that Saturn get in line with traditional ways of doing things.

That highlights one of the biggest challenges in leadership. Leaders have to choose between control and innovation. You can't have both. You can define the desired outcomes. You can create the boundaries, but you can't expect your team to be creative, innovative, or artistic if you try to control every element of the execution. If you must have full control, you just need to know that you are also choosing to shut down new ideas and innovations in your organization.

Unfortunately, the church is notorious for religiously keeping things the way they've always been but hoping we'll somehow achieve different results. Avoiding new approaches. Top-down, centralized leadership. Preserving the traditional ways of doing things. Sound familiar?

It's a great reminder that our past successes can be one of the greatest contributing factors to our future demise. GM used to have a winning formula. It worked in previous generations. Recently, though, it's not been working so well.

I used to drive a powder blue Chevy Impala. Thirty years ago that was a great ride. They may be coming out with some new, innovative automobiles now, but it wasn't too long ago that it seemed GM still wanted to make cars as though it were 1979 while expecting to get the same results. By sticking with that approach, they dropped from 45 percent of the market share thirty years ago to hovering around 20 percent today. In fact, back in 2008, Toyota ended GM's seventy-seven–year reign as the world's largest automaker.

It's easy to look at churches that might still be "driving the Chevy Impala" and easily draw conclusions for why they are in decline. Before you do that, though, I think it's good to remember that GM was once a very successful company. When you experience success, it's tough to let go. You want to control the formula because it works. You are reticent to try new approaches. The only problem is that eventually the world around us is going to change. When that happens, you, too, will be driving the Chevy Impala.

7

You Focus on Activities Instead of Outcomes

While many church leaders are full of vision and passion, they lack an effective strategy to accomplish their mission. That leads to a feeling of disorganization, and ultimately they feel stuck. When this happens, you'll spend more time focused on activities instead of outcomes. How do you know you're focused on activities? When you find yourself focusing on *bigger* versus *better.*

Truett Cathy, the founder of Chick-fil-A, said, "When we get better the customer will force us to get bigger!" In the church world, this means that we must take time to improve what we do, not just come up with bigger versions of what's mediocre. Instead of trying to outdo your last event, set design, or sermon illustration, get together with your team and improve the little things.

You've got too many ideas and too little action. It's more fun for leaders to brainstorm and dream, but that's not the hard work of the ministry. Real effectiveness comes when we organize volunteers around a mission, create processes to follow up with guests and givers, and lead our staff with intentionality and intensity. Visionary leaders often make the mistake of thinking that their church can grow on vision. While vision is helpful and necessary, getting organized may have more long-term positive effects.

At some point, you have to just do the hard work and stick with it. A quote from Calvin Coolidge noted in the program at his memorial service in 1933 described it this way:

Nothing in the world can take the place of persistence. Talent will not; nothing is more common than unsuccessful men with talent. Genius will not; unrewarded genius is almost a proverb. Education will not; the world is full of educated derelicts. Persistence and determination are omnipotent. The slogan 'press on' has solved and always will solve the problems of the human race.

Are you distracted? As a church leader, there are many things that you can do. Even good opportunities can side-track us from doing what matters most. Instead of chasing new opportunities, go to work on your worship services, children's ministry, and community service. Keep your eye on the ball. Don't let too many new ministry opportunities dilute your core purpose.

Stop and ask if the activities on your schedule contribute to, or support, your core values and mission. If you don't know your core values and mission, you've discovered one of your most glaring weaknesses!

8

You Fail to Equip God's People

It's easy to get caught in the trap of growing your staff without proportionately cultivating your volunteer assets. There are certain common refrains I hear as I'm talking with growing churches across the country. This is one of them—we fail to equip God's people to do the work of God.

I've heard many leaders in recent months acknowledge that they're trying to shift the ministry to volunteers rather than continuing to hire more staff. Likely, the economic challenges have precipitated that shift in strategy. Whatever the case, I think it's a good thing.

Eric Geiger offered this thought as it relates to engaging volunteers in ministry. He explains how pastors and other paid staff may actually be hampering spiritual growth by holding on to ministry:

> People who are gifted by God and called to serve Him are put on the bench as they watch the professional ministers make the ministry happen. Instead of fostering a serving posture among believers, this kind of "ministry" develops consumers. By keeping ministry from the majority of the people, they are taught to be moochers and consumers of the faith rather than participators and contributors. As their spiritual gifts go underutilized, they miss the joy of experiencing Christ by serving others.

Wondering where your church stands on this topic? Do a little math. Take the number of people who volunteer somewhere in ministry at any given time each month. Divide that by the total number of students and adults at your church. That'll give you a percentage. Here's my suggestion:

- If the percentage of students and adults serving is over 45 percent, you are in a healthy range for engaging volunteers in ministry.
- If you are in the 30- to 45-percent range, you're doing okay but there's room for improvement.
- If you are under 30 percent, you need a volunteer strategy adjustment.

With that in mind, Lifepoint Church in Fredericksburg, Virginia, needs to be on your radar. They've grown rapidly in recent years. But that's not what's most unique about this ministry.

What's unique about Lifepoint is their commitment to giving ministry away to volunteers. They have several strategies for making that happen, but let me highlight the most obvious one—they don't hire staff to *do* ministry.

Of all the churches I've worked with over the last couple of years, Lifepoint has the lowest staff-to-attendance ratio. They only have 1 full-time equivalent staff member (that includes all staff, not just ministry staff) for every 150 people in attendance. Only about 35 percent of their budget is spent on staff expenses.

Because they have very few staff, they are forced to empower volunteers to do the ministry. Almost 70 percent of their adults volunteer. That's the highest percentage of adults volunteering of all the churches I've worked with.

So, if you're following at home: Lifepoint has the record for the fewest staff compared to attendance, and they also broke the record for the most people volunteering. Coincidence? I don't think so.

This is another simple reminder that you can have a strong vision, but it's good systems and strategies that shift behaviors. This is just one example of that principle.

9

Your Ministries Ignore People Outside the Church

This excerpt from Jason Fried and David Heinemeier Hansson's book *Rework* keeps reverberating in my mind:

> *When you stick with your current customers come hell or high water, you wind up cutting yourself off from new ones. Your product or service becomes so tailored to your current customers that it stops appealing to fresh blood. And that's how your company starts to die.*

That's consistent with one of the key attributes of churches in decline. When churches become inward-focused and start making decisions about ministry to *keep* people rather than *reach* people, they also start to die. In Luke 15:4, Jesus said it this way:

> *If a man has a hundred sheep and one of them gets lost, what will he do? Won't he leave the ninety-nine others in the wilderness and go to search for the one that is lost until he finds it?*

Why do you think some churches slip into the mode where they're so focused on keeping people that they neglect trying to reach people who are outside the faith? As I was reading the Bible, I stumbled upon 1 Corinthians 10:33:

*I, too, try to please everyone in everything I
do. I don't just do what is best for me; I do what
is best for others so that many may be saved.*

Fascinating perspective, *isn't it?* Typically, we don't operate like that. We put personal conviction or preferences ahead of what may be best for others. Think about it . . .

- It isn't worship if the music is too loud or too fast or the wrong genre.
- It isn't discipleship if the content is delivered in a home or online instead of in a classroom.
- It isn't missions if we help a neighbor who has wealth instead of focusing on people who live in poverty.
- The message is good if it calls out the sin of *other* people, but we're offended when it's our sin.
- Rather than embracing the ministries that are impacting the most people, we want the church to embrace our personal projects and passions.
- We're more inclined to give when we can direct how the money is used.

Crazy! You'd think we'd be intentional about living out our faith to do what's best for others. Instead, we make ministry decisions to try to keep people happy. That's how we end up with churches full of happy Christians. That's why churches stop growing. We start doing church for us instead of trying to impact the lives of people outside our walls.

The reality is that if we're going to reach people outside the church and outside the faith, we're going to have to be uncomfortable. And, once we figure out what's best for others today, it'll be different tomorrow. That will involve change. That means we'll have to get uncomfortable again.

Let's face it. It's a lot easier doing ministry when our only goal is to keep people happy. Doing what's best for others makes life and ministry messy. We have to be willing to rock the boat. We have to be willing to watch people who don't have a "1 Corinthians 10:33" mindset leave the church.

When I stop doing what's best for me and focus on what's best for others, though, that's when real life-change happens. It's worth making "happy Christians" mad so that many may be saved.

People who walk through the doors of our church every Sunday may look okay on the outside, but many are dealing with some tough stuff on the inside. Addictions. Marriages collapsing. Kids heading in a wrong direction. Medical challenges. Financial crisis. Lack of purpose. Let me challenge you with these thoughts:

- When you teach on "felt needs," you aren't watering down the message. You are helping people find forgiveness and healing and a new direction for their life. It's easy to preach through the Bible. It's much harder to preach to hurting people who need to understand how the Bible applies to their lives.
- When the person sitting beside you is dealing with a marriage crisis that's leading to a crisis of faith, it makes your preferences of music and volume seem pretty insignificant.
- When you neglect the mission field in your neighborhood because of your sole desire to help people across the ocean, I wonder if you're just choosing the path of least resistance.
- When you choose to focus on your theological differences at the expense of helping people find healing and hope, could it be that you haven't spent enough time *living out* your faith because you're too busy *defending* your faith?

I've looked in people's eyes and heard many stories. They are the real stories of real people experiencing real pain. Let's not forget why we do what we do.

The end of this first section is only the beginning of your path to significant change. It's up to you what you decide to do with all of this. Maybe you say, "Forget it," put on your leisure suit, and head back to the 1970s. That's your prerogative. But if you're ready to shed the polyester and move on, great! Next we'll look at how to hang up the leisure suit for good.

Part Two

Hanging Up the Leisure Suit

How to Get Unstuck

10

How Do We Get Different Results?

Have you ever heard someone say, in one way or another, "I wouldn't be caught dead in that!" or a similar statement? Normally, such words are blurted out in reference to really bad attire, like a lime-green, 110 percent polyester leisure suit. But it's a tragedy when the "outfit" they're talking about is the local church.

As difficult, or daunting, as it may seem, we need to take a closer look at out-of-date, out-of-touch, or just plain every-day-as-normal church environments, systems, or tactics—basically the things that keep a church from moving forward. So many churches are stuck where they are, and if they even recognize this state of being, many don't know how to break free from the past and move ahead.

Don't feel too terrible if you feel that you are stuck right now. It happens to all of us—every person, every organization, every business—from time to time. Recognizing where you are is the first step, but then you must get moving to where God is calling you to be.

Getting unstuck is not about updating your Web site, becoming a more seeker-friendly congregation, changing the kind of worship songs (or hymns) you sing, or even what a leadership team structure should look like. Some of those things may need to be addressed, but only after you take a look below the surface to figure out why things are done a certain way and what God is calling you to do to live out the gospel message.

I probably shouldn't admit this, but sometimes it makes me feel better to know that other organizations are feeling the pain as well. For example Borders was in the news a lot when their business was dying. Early in 2011, the company announced they would be shutting down two hundred bookstores. Faced with liquidating $350 million of inventory, they were stuck . . . and unfortunately, they couldn't get *unstuck* and had to shut their doors for good, even though people are still reading books.

A couple of years ago, you and I became owners of General Motors. The U.S. government had to use a $50 billion (that's with a "b") bailout to keep the company afloat. Despite the government's help, GM's competitors continue to gain ground. People are still buying cars, but GM is stuck.

The United Methodist Church has lost about three million members since 1970. The number of people attending at least one Church of England service each month is down by 50 percent since 1968. Today less than 3 percent of the population attends services. Denominations rich in history are stuck.

I get to work with and communicate with church leaders across the country every day. Here's what I know to be true—churches all around you are stuck as well. Sometimes they don't know they're stuck, but the signs are fairly obvious. Here are some symptoms to identify whether or not *your* church is stuck. Some of them are more obvious than others:

- The church has stopped growing.
- People aren't accepting Christ and getting baptized.
- The congregation is aging.
- Giving has declined.
- Spiritual growth has stalled, and people are just "consuming" ministry.
- People aren't serving.
- People have stopped reaching their neighbors.

- The church isn't developing leaders.
- Communications are confusing and lack purpose.

One of the main reasons churches are stuck is because their systems and strategies are broken. As I mentioned earlier in this book, churches continue to use their same systems but hope and pray for different results. The only way to get different results is to engage different systems. Unfortunately, though, many churches—and, in fact, many denominations—would rather stay stuck and eventually die rather than make changes that might make people (including leaders) feel uncomfortable.

I've been reading through Exodus again in recent days. God had a plan for his people. He had a better place for them. Moses was called to lead the people to that better place. It was someplace the people had never been before. Though Moses was trying to lead the people by following God's plan, the whole congregation grumbled. It wasn't just some of the people grumbling—*everybody* grumbled. Sound familiar?

Where the first section of this book helped identify *why* your church is probably stuck, this section will discuss *how* you can turn things around and get *un*stuck. Maybe it would be a good idea, though, to start with a little self-assessment. Take a look at the bulleted list above. Are there any symptoms that might indicate your church is stuck? Be honest.

Jim Collins said this in *How the Mighty Fall:*

> *Those in power blame other people or external factors—or otherwise explain away the data— rather than confront the frightening reality that the enterprise may be in serious trouble.*

Now I'll ask again . . . where are you stuck?

11

Mind the Gap

If you've been to London, you're very likely familiar with "the Tube," which is what they call their subway system. Wherever you travel using the subway in London, you're always told to "mind the gap." You hear that phrase on the loudspeakers. You see that phrase plastered throughout the subways. You won't be in London very long before you're aware of the warning to mind the gap.

When you're traveling in London, "the gap" refers to the space between the subway platform and the train. As you're stepping out of the train, there's a caution to mind the gap between the train and the platform. It would be a bad day if you fell in the gap.

That word picture struck a chord with me, because I believe there's a gap that exists in churches today as well. In recent months, I've been warning church leaders to "mind the gap"—the gap between vision and the people who are waiting to execute that vision. Unfortunately, leaders with big vision tend to ignore the gap. They buy into the myth that if people unify behind a clear vision, the ministry will succeed. Let me explain why that type of thinking may lead to you getting stuck.

Today it's not uncommon for churches to have vision statements. Knowing the importance of unifying behind a clear vision, leaders have gone through many conversations and exercises to develop the church's vision statement. Let's look at an example. Let's assume our church's vision statement is to: "Love God. Love people. Change a community." That's a very compelling vision.

With their new vision statement completed, leaders will preach messages and create campaigns to gain support of the new vision. If the leader is effective in vision casting and has built trust, people will rally behind the vision and the leader. The vision statement may end up on the Web site, in the weekly bulletin or weekly newsletter, or on the walls of the church facilities. In fact, if the communications and vision casting strategy is executed effectively, it's possible for everyone in the church to know and embrace the vision of the church.

That's the problem. It's possible for everyone to know the vision but still not have any clue what they're supposed to do to help make the vision become reality. So how do you "mind the gap"? By focusing on specific strategies and systems that are established to accomplish the vision. Visually, it may look like this:

Vision + [Strategies & Systems] + Execution = Results

When churches end up just "doing church"—continuing to do what they have always done—the strategies and systems gap may seem wider and deeper than the Grand Canyon. A church may have a vision statement that is much different from that of the church down the street, and yet it still ends up employing the same methods used by its neighboring church. Many churches do this because no one takes the time to figure out what it will take to turn vision into reality. So in the end, churches end up doing the same things churches have always done but still hoping for—even expecting—different results.

Here are some warning signs that your ministry may not be minding the gap:

- Since you haven't clarified your strategies and systems, the loudest person decides what does or doesn't happen in your church.

- You are losing great staff and lay leaders to other churches or community organizations because you've not empowered them with clear strategies and systems.
- Because there's a gap, good people with good hearts are trying to fill the gap by developing their own strategies and systems to accomplish your vision, but you'll eventually have so many people pulling the church in different directions that it creates division or, ultimately, a church split.
- More meetings are required because you haven't clarified strategies and systems, so every time an issue pops up you have to reinvent the wheel. People who crave power love this because there are more meetings to make decisions. People who crave ministry impact, though, grow frustrated and leave the church.
- Your giving has plateaued or is declining. People support a vision when they know specifically how it is going to be accomplished, but people do not give to a vision statement simply because it's prominently displayed in literature or on a plaque somewhere.

If people are sitting on the sidelines and aren't engaged in ministry, that's a loud warning that you need to mind the gap. I'm sure they want to fully buy into your vision. And I'm certain they truly wish to invest their time and resources into executing it. If they're completely clueless as to what they're supposed to be doing, though, they'll continue sitting on the bench watching the game clock tick down to a certain loss.

In his book *The E-Myth Revisited*, Michael Gerber said it this way:

> *What makes people work is an idea worth working for, along with a clear understanding of what needs to be done.*

So what are you going to do to help people in your church get a clear understanding of what needs to be done? How are you going to establish a specific "minding the gap" strategy to accomplish your vision? What systems do you need to put in place today? Putting systems in place will make it possible for you to empower leaders and mobilize people. Without systems, you have to stay involved in every task and every decision.

So I already know what you're thinking. You're thinking, *This is a great business philosophy, but it has no place in my church. It's not biblical.* (In addition to minding the gap, I guess I can also read minds.) We'll cover biblical examples of ministry strategies and systems in the next chapter.

12

God Uses Systems to Accomplish His Purposes

I mentioned earlier in this book how churches often fall into the trap of trying to use their same systems over and over while hoping and praying for different results. Then I shared the importance of minding the gap in the last chapter—making sure the systems and strategies support the vision you're trying to accomplish.

Of course, as soon as I start to talk about systems and strategies, I'm sure questions start to surface: Doesn't God build the church? Where is the Holy Spirit involved? What about prayer? Aren't you embracing a business approach rather than a biblical model?

As I read through the Bible, I'm amazed at how God used systems to accomplish his purposes. Where God provides a vision, he also seems to provide a system or strategy to accomplish that vision. Let's look at some examples.

When God decided he needed to eliminate the wickedness that was pervasive in men's hearts across the earth, he sent a flood. But, before doing that, he gave Noah a system for building the ark so that he could redeem his people (see Genesis 6).

When Moses was chosen to lead God's people out of Egypt, he fell into the trap of attempting to do it all on his own. His father-in-law, Jethro, gave Moses a system for leadership structure to accomplish God's purposes (see Exodus 18).

When God wanted to rebuild the walls around Jerusalem, he chose Nehemiah to carry out the mission. Nehemiah had a challenge—he had to construct the wall while constantly being under the threat of enemy attack. Because of that, Nehemiah deployed a strategy where half the men worked rebuilding the wall while the other half stood on guard (see Nehemiah 4).

There are plenty of examples in the New Testament as well. For example, when Jesus empowered the twelve apostles to carry on his ministry, he gave them specific instructions on how to carry out that mission (see Matthew 10).

Then, when Jesus decided to send out seventy-two other disciples, he established a strategy for doing that in teams of two. It's as if Jesus knew he wanted to establish a model for team leadership from the very beginning (see Luke 10).

Later, as the early church was getting established, God gave Paul the mission of organizing and leading churches in the Roman empire. With that, Paul instructed Titus to establish a system of appointing elders in every town in Crete to encourage healthy churches (see Titus 1).

Of course, this is only a sample of the examples. When you study God's word further, you'll see how much more he used systems and strategies throughout history to accomplish his purposes. Among other things, though, here's what I believe we can learn from these examples:

- When God provides a vision for what he wants to accomplish, he many times provides a specific strategy for getting it done.
- There will be times when God gives vision to one person or team but uses the gifts of another person or team to develop and implement the strategy.
- Prayer is important, but God also calls us into action. God uses his people to fulfill his purposes.

I provided some examples of how God used systems to accomplish his purposes, but you may want to continue the conversation with your team. By studying this together, you may uncover principles you can apply to your church's systems to help you get unstuck.

13

Building a Healthy Foundation

When I start a church consulting engagement, I first make sure all the critical pieces for a healthy ministry are present. Second, I ask questions and review communications and practices to see what elements get the most focus.

I believe a healthy organization includes all six of these elements:

1. **Purpose**—This is the mission of the organization. Though all the other elements are required for a healthy organization, a clear purpose is the most important. Without this, the most common question is, "Why do we exist?"

2. **Strategy**—This is the current plan to carry out the purpose of the organization. It may (no, it *should*) change throughout the years. Without a strategy, the most common question is, "What should we do?"

3. **People**—You have to build a solid team to accomplish the purpose of your organization. Outside of the *why*, I believe *who* is the next most important aspect of a healthy organization. Without good people in the right roles, the most common question is, "Who is with us?"

4. **Structure**—The foundation and frame of your organization needs to support the strategy you

embrace. Just like the bone structure in our body changes as our bodies grow, a church's structure must stay fluid as the organization grows. Without structure, the most common question is, "Who is responsible?"

5. **Systems**—These are what clarify the processes for carrying out the strategy. Within a church, systems are the simple, replicable methods to help people move from where they are to where God wants them to be. Without them, the most common questions is, "How should we do this?"

6. **Metrics**—Numbers and heart-change stories provide the measure for whether or not the purpose is being accomplished. A lack of supporting data may mask an unhealthy organization even where life-change stories are prevalent. A lack of life-change stories may mask an unhealthy organization even when numbers look positive. Without both sets of metrics, the most common question is, "Are we accomplishing our mission?"

Now, as I mentioned, these elements are critical for organizational health, but not all of them are equal. I still believe the *purpose* has to be the priority. If that's not the case, the organization can become unbalanced and grow unhealthy.

For example, consider the organization that puts its people first. In those instances, I often see very inward-focused congregations that are not concerned with reaching people outside the faith. Instead, they make decisions based on the people who are already on the team or in the church.

Consider the organization that puts systems first. In those instances, where it's more about the systems, the focus is on following the rules. The rules overshadow the overall purpose, and sometimes the rules create barriers to accomplishing that purpose. This is the church that's concerned about following Robert's Rules of Order.

There's also the church that puts the strategy before the purpose. In those instances, the church is so concerned about making sure the strategy stays the same, that they are left behind as culture and people change. This is the church that wants to preserve the past.

Now it's your turn. With your leadership team, take this health assessment to see if these foundational aspects of a healthy organization are present in your ministry. Rate each of the six categories below based on this scale: (1) Strongly Disagree; (2) Disagree; (3) Neither Agree nor Disagree; (4) Agree; (5) Strongly Agree:

- We have clarified our unique purpose as a church, and it's the priority for all decisions.
- We have established a specific strategy to accomplish our purpose.
- We have the right people with the right strengths in the right roles.
- We have structured the organization around our ministry strategy.
- We have established systems that can be replicated to support the strategy.
- We have collected stories and data trends to confirm what we are doing actually works.

How did you do? Are there any elements that are missing in your ministry? Is something other than your purpose getting the most attention? If so, which one has the focus? Now do the same exercise for the core ministry areas of your church. In every ministry area, all the elements need to be present, but they should all support the overall purpose of the church.

14

When Teaching Creates Barriers to Change

One of the great myths in ministry is that we have the power to change behaviors by teaching more. We teach during worship services. We teach at student ministry gatherings. We teach at women's events. We teach at men's retreats. Even our small groups are built around teaching. We've fallen into the trap of thinking the only way people will take a next step is if we teach at them more.

My dad was a marching band director. Because of that, I grew up loving *The Music Man*. Harold Hill is nothing like my dad. Hill was a con artist. He really knew nothing about starting a marching band. All he wanted to do was sell band instruments and uniforms to make money. For his charade to work, he used the "think system" in order to train his musicians. Hill wasn't concerned about the kids learning the notes to become better musicians—he just encouraged them to *think* their way to becoming a marching band.

My dad's approach was very different. His system involved teaching, but it also included learning how to play each note, participating in personal lessons and practice, band rehearsals to fine-tune the music together, marching drills on the practice field, band camps to master the programs, warm-ups before each performance, etc. Dad implemented systems to support his teaching, and it resulted in an award-winning marching band that became known as the "Pride of Piqua."

If churches (and people) are going to get unstuck, we have to stop leaning so heavily on teaching to produce *all* the change, while beginning to create healthy systems to support the teaching. Within the context of a church, a healthy system is a simple, replicable process to help people move from where they are to where God wants them to be (one of the six elements of a healthy organization listed in the last chapter).

For example, if we want to move more people into serving others, not only should we teach them about what the Bible has to say on that topic, but we need to support that teaching with healthy systems to encourage people to take their next step, such as:

- Create ways to help people identify their gifts.
- Train people on how to "tap shoulders" of their friends to invite them into ministry.
- Establish "first serve" opportunities so there are obvious steps to get people serving.
- Streamline connection points with one, clearly marked place in your lobby and one, easy-to-find link on your Web site for people to sign up to serve.
- Eliminate competing events that deter people from serving.
- Reduce staff to increase the reliance on volunteers.

If your systems are broken or lacking, though, you can teach all you want . . . but it's not going to change behaviors.

Again, one problem I see in churches I work with is that they believe teaching *is* the system. When that happens, they begin to rely on what I've affectionately begun to call "The Funnel of Doom." The funnel works like this:

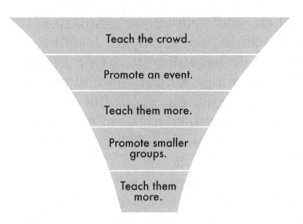

If we want to change behavior, we gather people on Sunday morning and teach them. Then we promote an event, where we try to gather people again. When we get people there, we teach them some more. Then we encourage people to gather in groups where—you guessed it—we attempt to teach them even more. And, along the way we grow frustrated because fewer people are actually taking each step. We blame it on people for not prioritizing their time and showing up. Maybe it's time we just acknowledge that The Funnel of Doom doesn't produce life change.

Don't misquote me on this. I really do believe that biblical teaching is a key component to encouraging life change. Jesus did it. He taught in front of crowds of thousands, but that was only one part of his ministry. His teaching was supported by faith steps, relationships, disciplines, and actions that led to a movement.

The problem occurs when teaching is not supported by healthy systems to encourage next steps and application of that teaching. Teaching alone promotes personality-driven ministries where people show up and listen . . . and that's about it. We need to create systems to encourage people to put what they learn into action.

Remember, your message has the potential to shift thinking. Your systems have the potential to shift behaviors.

15

Eight Characteristics of Healthy Systems

Throughout the previous five chapters, I've shared the importance of establishing healthy systems; discussed the fact that many churches have a gap between vision and execution; showed how, without healthy systems, they won't be able to accomplish God's vision for their ministry; and I've also explained that within the context of a church, a healthy system is a simple, replicable process to help people move from where they are to where God wants them to be.

Because your organization is unique, there's no way I can tell you specifically what systems you need in place to accomplish the vision God has for your church. I can, however, share some common characteristics of healthy systems that may point you in the right direction. With that in mind, here are eight characteristics of healthy systems for churches:

1. **They empower leaders to accomplish ministry without always having to get permission.**
   Without systems, every decision must go back to the senior pastor, the senior management team, the committee, etc. In his book *Making Ideas Happen*, Scott Belsky said it this way: "The more people who lie awake in bed thinking about your idea, the better. But people only obsess about ideas when they feel a sense of ownership." Good

systems will give leaders the freedom to make decisions within established boundaries.

2. **They are embraced and championed by the top leadership.** It does absolutely no good for systems to be established that top leadership doesn't support and encourage everyone to use. If the top leaders can't endorse the system, you're not ready to implement the system.

3. **They mobilize many people rather than leaning on a select handful of talented individuals.** If your system is "Contact Sue for more information," you don't have a system. If your system is "Go hear John teach on the topic," you don't have a system. You have some gifted individuals. Good systems point people to next steps (processes, tools, resources, etc.) rather than specific people.

4. **They simplify the path.** The objective is to create just enough of a framework to make it easier for people. Good systems are intuitive. Typically, the fewer the steps, the better the systems. If you want to improve a system, challenge your team to figure out how to reduce the steps required. And, whatever you do, make sure your "customer" doesn't have to guess where to go next.

5. **They are established around key touch points in your organization.** Think about your overall ministry. Do you want people to connect in ministry? Find a group? Communicate an event? Become a member? Join your staff? Those are all key touch points where people typically take a next step. Those are the places where you need strong systems.

6. **They improve over time.** If you feel like you have to wait until the system is perfect, you will stay stuck. You need to roll out the beta version. Test-drive it. See what works, and tweak the rest based on the feedback you receive.

7. **They need to change over time.** This is the challenge that many mainline churches are facing. They're still trying to use systems that worked years ago but are no longer effective today. It's a dangerous place when we start protecting the systems to the detriment of accomplishing the overall mission.

8. **They are measured and monitored for trends.** You'll need to capture both numbers and stories. The objective, though, is to look at outcomes (life change) rather than inputs (church activities).

Good people using bad systems will never produce good results. Normal people using good systems can produce great results.

If you were standing in the middle of a mud puddle, buried ankle (or knee) deep, the only way to get unstuck would be to move—to take that first step and keep on going. By now, I'm sure you have a very good idea of how stuck you are, and you may have some initial thoughts about what you need to do now. The first step toward freedom from past systems, programs, structure, etc., is to allow this message to get personal. If you're not already doing so, consider going through this book with your leadership team. Use the discussion questions at the back to help you move toward becoming the church God is calling you to be.

In the next section we'll turn our attention to how you lead when you're off the platform, Monday through Saturday. Why do we often insist on wearing the same leadership style and listening to the same leadership "tunes" over and over when they're so out of date and out of touch with reality? I hope you will consider how effective you are in your role and decide what leadership changes are long overdue.

Part Three

Stayin' Alive

Build a Legacy of Leadership

16

What Will Be Your Leadership Legacy?

There's nothing quite like a leisure suit, is there? With that sentence read, I probably lost you for a few moments as pictures popped into your head. Maybe of a suit you had to wear as a child. Or one that your father used to wear way too often. But I bet there is no more memorable leisure suit than the eye-blinding white number John Travolta wore in the 1977 blockbuster *Saturday Night Fever.* And now I'm sure the song "Stayin' Alive" is stuck in your head too. Sorry!

That movie is a classic, but I bet you haven't watched it in years, if ever. And it's probably been a while since you wore a leisure suit or listened to that Bee Gees music unless you recently attended a 70s-themed party. It's all nostalgia—that's it! People from this era like to talk about the music and the clothing, but they don't want to live there anymore. And if they did, others would think they are crazy.

Reading the headlines in recent days, I was reminded of how vulnerable our legacies can be. It's challenging to see ministries that once had a huge impact finding themselves marginalized or on the verge of extinction.

I started to think about some of the similarities that appear to be consistent in these stories. Like the "check engine" light in your car, the following warnings may be signs that your legacy is at risk:

- *You talk about leadership but are unintentional about leadership development.* Attending (or speaking at) conferences and reading (or writing) leadership books is not enough. Is there a path in place to help young, gifted leaders grow and gain responsibility and authority over time?
- *Your success rests on the shoulders of one personality.* As I get older, I become more and more convinced that God designed us to be in community and for ministry to be accomplished in teams. That includes leading the ministry. Is there any one person who, if he left for an extended period of time, would put your organization at risk?
- *You begin making decisions based on past success rather than present reality.* Rarely do organizations spend themselves into a turnaround. If your ministry isn't having the same impact it experienced in the past, are you addressing leadership, vision, or strategy gaps, or are you trying to buy a better future?
- *You avoid the truth about the health of your organization.* It's one of the risks of never considering "the numbers." If you ignore or explain away trends over time, how in the world will you know if what you're doing is actually working?
- *You would rather close your doors than make uncomfortable changes.* It truly amazes me. I routinely see churches holding on to practices that aren't prescribed in Scripture, even if it jeopardizes their very existence. With the exception of rare instances, do your personal preferences almost always trump ministry impact?
- *You invest more effort in public perception than in private integrity.* It doesn't matter how gifted the leader or how God-ordained the vision or how effective the strategy—in the end, our personal and

relational health will make or break our legacy. Are your personal disciplines and priorities establishing the foundation for future ministry impact?

One generation of ministry doesn't make a legacy. What are you doing to prepare the next generation for continued impact? Leadership expert John Maxwell says that "everything rises and falls on leadership." I hope this book injects new life and ideas into your life and ministry so the legacy of your leadership remains alive and well for generations to come.

17

Are You Really the Leader?

One Friday night my son, Jacob, had a basketball game so the whole family went to watch. Midway through the game, our then-four-year-old Brooke started pestering her sister Abby, who was eight at the time, which went on for quite some time. Now, Abby has great patience, but she's also very human and . . . a few minutes later she basically kneed Brooke in the chest.

I guess as the father I was supposed to reprimand Abby for that reaction, but I didn't. Brooke immediately started yelling at her sister and letting the whole gymnasium know that she had been wronged. Because I thought I would have reacted the same way Abby did, I decided to just pick up the little, agitating twerp and plop her a safe distance from Abby.

At that point, Brooke folded her arms across her chest, looked me square in the eyes, and said in the sternest voice a little girl could muster, "You're not in charge of me." What do you do in a situation like that? I just snickered and then reminded my wife that Brooke was *her* daughter.

Let me just clarify for you that I am, indeed, Brooke's father. I'm the leader—at least on paper. Just because I have positional leadership in our family, though, doesn't necessarily mean I'm always the leader in my kids' eyes.

The same thing is happening on a different scale in organizations everywhere. People are in positional leadership roles who aren't necessarily the leaders of their organizations. The days are behind us for those situations when someone gets out of line and the head-honcho just takes their subordinate out to the woodshed for a reminder of *who's the boss.* Leadership is no longer a title on a business card. (Do people still carry those things?)

Leadership looks a lot different these days.

- It doesn't necessarily reside in the corner office.
- It's something that's earned rather than bestowed.
- It rarely tells people what to do, but rather asks, "How can I serve?"
- It can't be bought, because most people ultimately care very little about the money.
- It's focused more on the mission than the tasks.
- It's concerned more about fostering influence instead of wielding power.
- It recognizes the next new idea will come from someone else.
- It doesn't necessarily require words.

I'm hopeful that one of these days Brooke will acknowledge and respect my leadership in her life. Needless to say, we both probably have some maturing to do before that comes to fruition. Until then, I may need to remind her from time to time who's in charge. As long as she's a little girl, I think that strategy is going to work. When she becomes a teenager, probably not so much.

One generation of ministry doesn't make a legacy. What are you doing to prepare the next generation for continued impact?

18

Management Is Not Leadership

I recently read Anne Jackson's book *Mad Church Disease.* In it, she quotes Wayne Cordeiro, the senior pastor of New Hope Christian Fellowship in Oahu, Hawaii, whose words keep reverberating through my brain. In describing some practices he changed as a result of dealing with ministry burnout, he offered this:

> *I've learned that God has made me to be*
> *a leader, not a "manager." I was pulled in to*
> *"managing" for a few years as my main course.*
> *That diminished my leadership immune system,*
> *and I became susceptible to contagious maladies*
> *such as discouragement, exasperation, and being*
> *demotivated by others.*

There is a distinction between leading and managing. They are two entirely different roles. Both are valuable to an organization, but rarely is a person gifted to both lead and manage. They are typically wired up to do one or the other.

In their book, *First, Break All the Rules*, Marcus Buckingham and Curt Coffman defined both roles like this:

- **Managers**—"Great managers look *inward.* They look inside the company, into each individual, into the differences in style, goals, needs, and motivation of each person. These differences are small, subtle, but great managers need to pay attention to them. These subtle differences guide them toward the right way to release each person's unique talents into performance."

- **Leaders**—"Great leaders look *outward*. They look out at the competition, out at the future, out at alternative routes forward. They focus on broad patterns, finding connections, cracks, and then press home their advantage where the resistance is weakest. They must be visionaries, strategic thinkers, activators. When played well, this is, without doubt, a critical role. But it doesn't have much to do with the challenge of turning one individual's talents into performance."

The Bible also distinguishes these two roles. The spiritual gift of leadership found in Romans 12:8 is very different from the spiritual gift of management (or administration) found in 1 Corinthians 12:28. Few people have both of these gifts, but both are needed within a healthy church body.

If we are trying to be a manager when we're actually a leader, we will be unfulfilled and face ministry burnout as Wayne described. Likewise, if we're forced into a leadership role when we're actually a manager, we will face the same challenges.

I consider this a big topic that churches, generally, have failed to address. I challenge you to prayerfully consider this in the coming days for yourselves and your teammates. The health of your ministry, both personal and corporate, is at stake. And, while you're at it, invite your ministry team to press into this conversation as well.

Here's a simple exercise you can do with your leadership team. List every staff member or key volunteer. Next to each name, label the person as a leader, a manager, or a doer. Force yourself to put people in only one category based on their primary bent. Then ask yourselves: Are the right people in the right roles? Do we have the right mix? Are there any gaps?

Take a staff meeting to discuss the differences and challenge your team to make sure they are in a position that best reflects the way God created them . . . whether they are leaders, managers, or neither. God wants you serving where he designed you to be serving; to do otherwise is to disobey God.

19

Micromanagement Hurts Everyone

Typically, leaders are control freaks. They want the whole picture. They want to know the end game. The problem is, of course, most times that's not how God operates. God wants us to hear from him and trust him enough to be willing to just take the very next step.

Joshua and the Israelites were camped along the Jordan River, which was at flood stage. As if that wasn't enough of a challenge, he then informed this large group of people, "You have never gone this way before." Talk about a change management challenge!

At this point, God tells Joshua to send the priests out ahead with the ark of the covenant. He also explains that as soon as the priests take their first step into the river, the water will part. Everyone will be able to cross on dry land.

So let me summarize where we are at this point:

- We have a leader.
- The leader is trying to take a large group of people to a place they've never seen before.
- There are what appears to be insurmountable barriers in the way.
- Then you have God telling the leader to do something that's going to require a miracle.

If you ask me, this is not only a leadership crisis—this is a crisis of faith. Or maybe I'm just interpreting it that way because I know *me* too well. Here's what I don't like about who I am—I always want to know where I'm going to end up. I like to be in control. And micromanaging comes easy to me. The problem is that God typically doesn't operate that way.

God: *"Put your foot into the water."*

Tony: *"I've never put my foot into the water before."*

God: *"You need to put your foot into the water."*

Tony: *"If I do that, what's my next step?"*

God: *"I'll reveal that after you put your foot into the water."*

Tony: *"I want to know where I'm going to end up?"*

God: *"Don't you trust me?"*

We may *say* that we trust God to lead us where he wants us to go and to do what he wants us to do, but when we micromanage, we communicate something quite different. When I get together with leaders around the country, our conversation often takes us to the leadership trap. You've probably experienced this before. It's that feeling in your gut that says:

"IF I DON'T DO IT, NO ONE WILL."

Every leader experiences it—especially in ministry where we're dependent on volunteers to carry out the mission. Either we have the sense that nothing will be accomplished if we are not doing it ourselves . . . or, at least, that it won't be done right. Here's what's crazy about that. Your mind says it's true, but it's actually a lie. Here's the truth:

"IF I DO IT, NO ONE WILL DO IT."

Did you catch that? Whenever you decide to step in and do it, you're taking away the opportunity for someone else to do it. Whenever you step in to *do it right,* you're denying the opportunity for someone else to do it better. Until we embrace that reality, our impact and influence as a church will be limited.

What type of leader are you going to be? Are you going to deny the power of God working through others, or are you going to empower people to live out their God-given purpose?

20

Consensus Sucks

I'm growing more and more convinced that the worst thing an organization can do is try to reach a consensus about something. Think government. Think church committee meetings. Think declining big business.

On the surface, reaching a consensus seems like a positive thing because it means people have agreed to move in the same direction. That's a good thing isn't it? Before you answer that, consider these . . .

5 Reasons Why Consensus Sucks

1. *Consensus embraces the status quo.* It's human nature to prefer that things remain the same. So, when people get together to discuss the possibility of doing something a little different, it's normal for the majority to avoid making changes.

2. *Consensus gives malcontents an equal voice.* When everyone gets an opportunity to speak into the decision-making process, even the negative, bitter folks who don't embrace the vision have the opportunity to pull the rest of the group away from what would be best.

3. *Consensus short-circuits the radical ideas that lead to the biggest breakthroughs.* The big, bold ideas won't see the light of day. Yet those are the ideas that could potentially lead to the best innovations.

Consensus brings people back to the middle where the majority resides but mediocrity reigns.

4. *Consensus leaves unresolved conflict on the table.* At the opposite ends of a decision are distinct opinions that, if left unresolved, could potentially lead to division.

5. *Consensus discourages people from dreaming big dreams.* Want to neuter the creative thinkers, entrepreneurs, and visionaries in your organization? Though they make you uncomfortable and drive you crazy, they'll just go work someplace else if you keep forcing them to compromise their dreams.

In an interview with the *Economist* (April 2010), Ed Catmull, president of Pixar, talked about how managers like to be in control. He said that any manager has to get over this feeling quickly if he or she is going to survive in that role.

> *The notion that you're trying to control the process and prevent error screws things up. We all know the saying "It's better to ask for forgiveness than permission," . . . but I think there is a corollary: If everyone is trying to prevent error, it screws things up. It's better to fix problems than to prevent them. And the natural tendency for managers is to try and prevent error and over plan things.*

Things happen out of order all the time, Catmull says. And nothing goes as planned within churches, as I'm sure *you* have discovered. What consensus is for the most part—almost all the time—is an attempt to overly manage outcome, which unfortunately holds you back from going to where God wants you to move.

What do you think? Do you agree? Or, have you actually seen consensus work? What would you add or delete from the list? Let's try to reach a consensus on whether or not consensus sucks.

21

Stop Doing Ministry

I'm guessing you're familiar with the story from Acts 6 where the widows in the church were not getting fed. That's a bad situation. I know how grumpy I get when I'm hungry. I can't imagine how grumpy a group of hungry, older women can be. That can't be good.

These widows weren't getting fed because the apostles were not getting the job done. These leaders were supposed to be focusing on prayer and teaching God's Word (see Acts 6:4), but instead they were stuck trying to pull off a not-very-effective food distribution effort.

So who was at fault? It could have been the people in the church who were just showing up for services on Sunday morning but not engaging in ministry. Maybe they hadn't studied the Bible enough to learn that it's not biblical to pay pastors to do all the ministry of the church.

It could have been the fault of the leaders. Maybe they had fallen into the "I can do it better" trap. Maybe they weren't really leaders, so they weren't spiritually gifted to empower other people in ministry.

Either way, here's what strikes me about this passage. The apostles were engaged in ministry. In that day, food distribution was just as much a part of the ministry of the church as praying and teaching. They were doing ministry; they just weren't doing the *right* ministry. In other words . . .

It's possible to do the work of God without doing the work God has called you to do. That should be alarming for us. Because as the church grows, it requires us to prayer-fully consider questions like this:

- Am I encouraging people to serve in ministry?
- Am I helping people determine their gifts?
- Am I empowering new leaders?
- Am I a leader, or am I just in a leadership position?
- Am I doing what God designed me to do?

Fortunately, the apostles decided to empower seven other leaders to take responsibility for the food distribution. That allowed the apostles to get back to focusing on prayer and the teaching of God's Word. I guess you could say they stopped doing ministry and encouraged others to do it instead. As a result, "God's message continued to spread. The number of believers greatly increased in Jerusalem, and many of the Jewish priests were converted, too" (Act 6:7).

People pay me to figure this out for them, but let me share this advice for free: If you're doing *everything*, you're probably going to lead a small, ineffective ministry that's not consistent with God's plan for your life. So what are you going to do? You can continue to do the work of God, or you can . . .

Do the work God called you to do!

22

Focus on the Team, Not Your To-Do List

If you're the "complete the right task" type of leader, you better be extremely smart. You'll need to know how to do everything. Then you'll have to make sure your subordinates know how to do everything too. You'll be the one that has to come up with all the ideas. You'll be the person that is responsible for policing the troops to make sure they're staying in line. Ironically, if something goes wrong, you'll probably blame it on people.

If you're the "find the right people" type, you are constantly trying to build the right team and then get out of the way. When you have talented people around you, you don't need to know all the answers. The team generates the ideas, so it's not all on your shoulders. The right people are as concerned about the mission as you are, so you don't have to spend time keeping them in line. If something goes wrong and you have a great team, you see it as a systems or communications problem rather than a people problem.

Not getting the results you desire? Maybe it's time for a little self-assessment. Look at the diagram below to determine what path you are on. You may want to change your leadership focus.

Complete the Right Task	Hire the Right People
Hire someone willing to show up to work by 8:30 a.m. every morning. Give them specific tasks to complete with instructions on how they should do them. Routinely check up on them to make sure they're doing their job correctly. Periodically ask for their input to give them the impression they have a say in what happens. Provide bonuses to the people who get the most tasks right.	Build a team more talented than you. Define the end goal and the current objectives and give them the freedom to make it happen. Routinely monitor the metrics to make sure they're hitting the mark. Create space to let them dream and implement new ideas. Hold on to the all-stars and make sure they're compensated appropriately.

Part of the discussion I once had with some coaching network guys was related to the differences between empowerment and delegation. We took about fifteen minutes to brainstorm a list of the differences between the two. Here's part of where we landed:

Delegation: Here's what I need from you.
Empowerment: What do you need from me?

Delegation: This is how you do it.
Empowerment: This is your role.

Delegation: This is what I want it to look like.
Empowerment: This is where we're going.

Delegation: This is what you need to do next.
Empowerment: This is how it fits in the big picture.

Delegation: I'll give you the last 5 percent.
Empowerment: I'll let you contribute the last 5 percent.

Delegation: I own it.
Empowerment: You own it.

Delegation: Here's where I see this going.
Empowerment: Where do you see this going?

Delegation: Concrete.
Empowerment: Fluid.

Delegation: Toe the company line.
Empowerment: Pushback is encouraged.

Delegation: Tasks.
Empowerment: Results.

Delegation: No room for other leaders.
Empowerment: Room for other leaders.

Delegation: Guided by preference.
Empowerment: Guided by values.

Delegation: Here's my opinion.
Empowerment: What's your opinion?

Here's the reality: empowering other leaders is the way to build healthier organizations. It will be messier along the way, but you will end up in a place where your organization can have a much bigger impact and more people will be fulfilled in their roles.

23

Don't Lead Everyone in the Same Way

I've had the opportunity to lead a number of creative people over the last fifteen years both in ministry and in the marketplace. And, from time to time, I've been known to be a "creative" myself. Creatives are different. They deliver new ideas and approaches, but they come with their quirks. You can't lead creatives like you lead "normal" people.

Within the church, don't assume creative people only work in your worship arts area. They're likely to hang out there, but it's also very possible they're on just about every ministry team at your church. They may not sing songs or draw pictures, but they're still creative. And if you don't learn how to lead them, they'll find someplace else to take their creativity.

Here are some tips for leading creative people:

1. Tell them what to do, but not how to do it. You can hold them accountable for the results, but don't force them to embrace a certain process.

2. If you want their input, you'll need to ask. If you stop asking, they'll stop contributing.

3. If you ask, you better consider their input. If you're not really going to use their input, it's better not to even ask.

4. Know that they'll be emotionally attached to what they create. So, if you decide not to use their creation, you'll have to process that appropriately and not abruptly.

5. You need to give them a deadline, but it better be reasonable. Creative people need room to dream and let their ideas percolate.

6. Don't try to motivate them with money, but they do want your praise. They'll react when the extrinsic rewards are taken away, but they're really intrinsically motivated.

7. They'll get easily bored if they find themselves stuck in a routine/maintenance role. They need the freedom to take on new challenges and opportunities.

8. They deliver new ideas, but they dread the details. To bring the best out of them, you need to protect them from the bureaucratic structure and administrative tasks.

9. They need a creative and participative environment. Creative people need the fuel that other creative people generate.

10. You need to provide boundaries, but they need to experience freedom. Boundaries force people to get creative. That's when the best ideas are generated. But if creative people ever feel restrained, at best they'll start to sulk and at worst they'll join another team.

Do you consider yourself to be a creative person? If so, think about the best leader you've worked for. What did he or she do that brought the best out in you? Do you lead creative people? If so, think about your most creative people on the team. How do you lead them differently to get the biggest impact from their contributions? Let's get creative about leading creative people.

24

Don't Focus on Fixing Your Boss

It may or may not surprise you that the most frequently asked questions I receive is, "How do I change my boss?"

In a couple of instances where I knew the person was married, I responded to that question with this question: *How do you change your spouse?* (Hint for marital bliss: Don't try to answer that question. You'll find yourself sleeping on the couch tonight.) If you've been married longer than a few weeks, you know that you can't change your spouse. You're really fighting a losing battle if you think you will.

You can't change your spouse. You can't change your boss. The only person you have any hope of changing is yourself—and that, I've learned, is a little difficult without a move of God. It could quite possibly be the case that if you think your boss needs to change, maybe your perspective needs to change. Here are some ideas to consider:

- *Look in the mirror.* You may be thinking your boss is unhealthy, but is it possible that you're the one who really needs to make some changes? That's the easiest place to start.
- *Support your boss.* He or she is human. Your boss is learning how to lead just as you are. How can you provide encouragement? What can you do to make his or her life easier? Have you prayed for your boss recently?

- *Model healthy leadership.* If it works for you, and people acknowledge that you're helping the organization fulfill its mission, others may want to learn from you.
- *Focus on the relationship.* People don't like change unless they're initiating the change. None of us like being changed or receiving change. We all need relationships with people we can trust, though. It's amazing what you're willing to do for someone you trust.
- *Move on.* If you can't support your boss, then you're only pulling yourself and others down by sticking around. (Before you do that, though, make sure you've worked through the first four bullets above.)

I know. This is easy for me to write since I've worked for some great bosses along the way. I've been pretty fortunate. That said, we all face instances in even the healthiest of relationships where there is tension. The natural reaction is to want to fix the other person. Just thought it would be helpful for you to know . . .

You can't fix your boss! . . . But you *can* do a little coaching (even if you do it covertly). But also remember that if you *are* THE BOSS, there may be people out there who want to fix you.

25

Are You Comfortable Being Uncomfortable?

During a worship service a few years ago, we had an older couple, probably in their sixties, accept Christ. That's worth celebrating. I love to watch life change happen. Here's what's amazing about that—our services aren't designed for people in their sixties.

Our services are designed for a much younger audience. It's an audience that loves loud music. Most people who attend it are comfortable with video teaching, because video is already a huge part of their lives. They love the coffeehouse atmosphere.

Here's what we've learned. If we design our service experiences for a younger audience, we're more likely to reach that younger person *and* we'll also reach older folks. The reverse is not true. If we designed our service experience for an older audience, the younger crowd would not show up.

Now, here's the reality. Most churches in America are designed for an older audience. In fact, the more-seasoned folks in those churches are sitting on committees telling the students and young adults how they can and can't do ministry. The result? Younger people are leaving churches in droves.

Here's what I know to be true. As a leader, if I'm going to see the church continue to reach the next generations, I must:

- Give leadership to people younger than I . . . and let them make mistakes.
- Let younger folks lead me in worship . . . even when it's not my favorite style of music.
- Embrace new methods of ministry . . . even when it makes me uncomfortable.
- Pray and encourage and *finance* the next-generation church . . . and stop trying to make church a place that I would like to attend.

It's not about me. It's about the people who desperately need to know the hope, love, and forgiveness found only in Jesus Christ. For the ministry of the local church to remain effective, I need to be a leader who is comfortable with being uncomfortable.

In the last section of this book, we'll move from how you lead during the week to what you say Monday through Saturday. As you ponder the challenging ideas, helpful tips, and probing questions at the end of the book, take time to think through how you can change your conversations— that you'll start taking your weekday message as seriously as you do the Sunday sermon.

Part Four

Get Your Groove On

Communicate Through Change

26

All Churches Are Marketing

As a pastor or leader in your church, you focus most of your time and energy on Sundays—especially what will be heard that day. You need a compelling topic, relevant Scripture, relatable anecdotes, music that moves hearts toward God, motivation for people to give of their resources, etc. But what are people hearing the rest of the week?

What you say Mondays through Saturdays is vital to the success of your Sundays. Like it or not, the message you send out during the week—good or bad, spoken or unspoken—is marketing at its core. Now, before that freaks you out too much, think about it. If you believe in the gospel message, including the Great Commission, don't you want to get more people to come through your doors on Sunday to hear the Good News?

I'm a huge proponent of church marketing. Why? Because I happen to believe more is better. More people hearing the Gospel is better. More people taking steps in their spiritual journey is better. More people experiencing life change is better. More people having healthy marriages is better. More people finding God's purpose for their lives is better.

You may be saying, "My church doesn't embrace the marketing tactics of corporate America." Well, I doubt that very seriously. Whether you want to admit it or not, churches have been marketing for a long time, but you may have just never noticed it.

Have you seen church signs with clever clichés posted on them? (Marketing.) What about announcements for upcoming events communicated through church bulletins and newsletters, local newspapers, Internet searches, and word of mouth? (Yep, marketing.)

The experience a church creates, intentional or not, for first-time guests is also a form of marketing. So is how leaders interact with people who want to commit to taking their next step in their faith or in ministry partnership. Marketing is also evident in the environment of a church's meeting place as well as in its name and logo.

You may not see it as such, but it's marketing. All of that and more lead to impressions people have of your church. Whether you like it or not, these messages help people decide whether or not they will connect with your ministry.

In a blog post once, I told readers to stop marketing. The only problem with that advice is that it's not possible. I've never seen a church that wasn't marketing itself in some form or fashion. Go ahead. Try to prove me wrong. You won't be able to do it.

With that, I'd like to suggest that if we're going to embrace marketing, then there are strategies we can engage to make our marketing more effective.

27

When Does Church Marketing Work?

Church marketing is more effective when we realize it has little to do with advertising or promotion and when we focus less on what we say and more on how we act. Every interaction reflects the values we embrace, so make sure the message people hear is personal, biblical, excellent, relevant, simple, and so forth.

One important thing to realize is that if people aren't hearing your message, it most likely won't be clearer if you just say it louder. Instead of turning up the volume, make sure you're communicating the right message. Focus on building relationships instead of sharing information. Talk less about how great you are ("organization-focused") and more about life change ("people-focused").

You cannot force people to think about what they need until they know they need it, so get to know individuals, families, and their needs. Then reduce the number of competing messages you communicate so neither you nor others get distracted from what's vital. When communicating to those who are not yet regular attenders, make sure you:

- Know who you are trying to reach.
- Acknowledge that you can't reach everyone.
- Develop a way to measure the outcomes of your efforts.
- Deliver on what you promise.

Usually when you approach marketing with a marketing mindset, that's when messages are unfocused and ineffective. When you approach marketing with a focus on people and their needs, though, you'll notice that you're finally saying all the right things at just the right time and in the best way possible.

28

10 Ways to Improve Marketing without Spending Any Money

One day I started thinking about the constraints that we have as churches given today's current economic conditions. With that in mind, I began to brainstorm ways we can continue to improve how we communicate with the people we are trying to reach without spending any money. These are solutions that any church of any shape and size should be able to engage.

1. *Improve guest services on Sunday mornings.* Stress that Sunday mornings are a time for your hospitality team to be focused on visitors. The number one reason people will come back to your church is if they find the church to be friendly.

2. *Follow through with your promises.* If someone volunteers to take a next step in a group, serving, or attending an event, make sure the process is in place to follow up in a timely and personal fashion.

3. *Make it easy for people to ask questions.* Create a one-stop location, physical or online, where visitors can receive more information about your church.

4. ***Create ministry environments that compel people to invite their friends.*** Excellent preaching and worship music is not enough. Every environment in the church needs to create an opportunity for life change. When that happens, you won't be able to stop folks from inviting their friends.

5. ***Embrace social media.*** Facebook, Twitter, and blogs are an easy way to engage people in conversation and develop relationships. As relationships are developed, you'll earn the credibility to encourage people to take next steps.

6. ***Be different.*** Begin an unexpected series, have a unique worship experience, or do something (good) that gets people talking.

7. ***Make your church an active part of the community.*** Open your campus to the community, but also get engaged outside the walls of the church where you can directly impact people's lives.

8. ***Eliminate the noise.*** Prioritize what needs to be communicated. Eliminate competing messages. Stop the spam. The fewer the messages we deliver, the more likely the important messages will be heard.

9. ***Encourage word-of-mouth marketing.*** The number one reason people will show up to your church for the very first time is because someone invites them. If you have stopped growing, your very first question should be this: *Why have people stopped inviting their friends and what would have to happen for that to change?*

10. *Lead by example.* Although leading a church can become all-encompassing, find a way to cultivate personal relationships with nonbelievers. I know of a student who refused to walk through the doors of the church until her youth pastor, who got to know her at an outreach event, wrote her a two-line note thanking her for being a part of the youth group.

Have you used any of these strategies? What was the outcome? And do you have any other free marketing ideas that you'd like to share?

29

What's in a Name?

Remember the line from *Romeo and Juliet:*

*"What's in a name? That which we call a rose
By any other name would smell as sweet."*

So what's in a name? It's an interesting question. For those of us responsible for branding, we take names seriously. Honestly, though, I'm more and more of the opinion that names mean very little. In other words, a brand by any other name would smell as sweet.

For example, do people order Tall, Grande, and Venti coffee drinks on a daily basis because they are made by a company named Starbucks, or do they purchase them because they expect to always get a quality beverage? Do people go to Cirque du Soleil because the performance is presented by an organization called Cirque du Soleil or because people know they're going to experience a phenomenal performance from Cirque du Soleil? Do people use Google search because the application is offered by a company called Google or because people know they're going to get accurate search results from Google? Do you see my point?

It's not the name. It's the quality of the product or service or the experience that matters.

So, in our case, I don't think people attend a specific church because it's called by a certain name. But, when people expect something unique on Sundays and know the impact of that experience, they will attend. Same principle holds for every other ministry or environment within our church. People don't connect or participate or invite their friends because of the name of the ministry. Those results happen because of the experience and the life change those ministries and environments produce.

In other words, the name doesn't matter until the brand is established. If the product or service generates positive results over a period of time, people will begin to associate the name with a perceived expectation of results. When that happens, the name matters. That's the "Kool Aid" moment.

When people love the product or service enough based on previous experiences to "drink the Kool Aid," the name matters. That's when someone buys a computer just because Apple made the computer. But, even in this case, people didn't arrive at the Kool Aid moment because of the name. They got there because of the quality of the product or service or experience.

Though names don't generate new customers, they can filter out prospective customers.

So, what do you think? Would that which we call a rose by any other name smell as sweet?

30

Why Churches Should Stop Marketing . . . for a Moment

I know this sounds a bit drastic, but there is method to my madness, so please hear me out on this topic. Here's why I believe that *it's not about your marketing.*

One of the reasons why I hate it when other churches try to mimic another church's success is that they try to copy the tactics instead of the core objective, which is to help people enter into a relationship with Jesus and take steps in their walk with Christ. When life change happens, people talk. When people talk, more people show up.

My concern, though, is that we jump to marketing tactics too quickly. We think if we're going to get a crowd, we need to market it more. That's lazy thinking, and part of my fear, frankly, is that our marketing may actually work. If we haven't asked the right questions first, the people who show up may find that what we're marketing is vastly different from what they experience.

That's why I think churches should stop marketing. No, maybe not forever. Maybe not even beyond your next ministry team meeting. I think it would be healthy, though, for you to take marketing tactics completely off the table for a moment and ask challenging questions such as these:

- If we stopped marketing, what would we have to change for people to invite their friends?
- If we stopped marketing, would the environment make people want to come back?

- If we stopped marketing, would the conversation be relevant to people's lives?
- If we stopped marketing, would the relationships keep people connected?
- If we stopped marketing, would the next step be obvious?
- If we stopped marketing, would people still believe in and be excited about our "brand"?
- If we stopped marketing, might we actually help remove some of the noise from people's lives?
- If we stopped marketing, would we get a better response when we start using marketing tactics?
- If we stopped marketing, are we more likely to be sensitive to God's leading?

The point here is that we're trying to fix the problem by playing the marketing card. Direct mail won't fix your problem. Billboards won't fix your problem. Neither will platform announcements or bulletin ads or bumper stickers. If you don't address the more challenging questions listed above, good marketing will just help an unhealthy organization fail faster.

31

The LOUDER Trap!!!!

When I was taking piano lessons early on in life, I had a bad habit of pounding on the keys. In music terms, I loved *fortissimo*. "Very loud" came very easy to me. Then my piano teacher taught me the value of dynamics. She explained how beautiful music isn't just achieved by hitting the right notes–it's also a reflection of the dynamics. The power of *fortissimo* doesn't grab our attention in music unless we also embrace the *pianissimo*, the very soft movements.

Have you ever been in public when a parent blows a gasket and starts yelling at their child but gets no response? Here's my bet. The very first time the parent reacted like that, their child responded. The reason why kids choose to ignore a yelling parent is because it's a learned response. Kids are smart. It doesn't take them long to learn that if a parent constantly yells but never follows through with any real punishment, then they can ignore the screams.

Loud is only effective when it's louder than normal. If it's always loud, then loud becomes the new normal. In other words, loud is not loud anymore.

The same principle holds when we're trying to promote something in ministry. Here's how it works. You commit to a promotions campaign to get people to a new series or a big event. You decide to go loud. You buy the billboards, print the fliers, hang the banners, create the viral videos, and announce to the world, "This is going to be the best deal ever!" That's great. The first time it may work. And, chances are it could work, again, sometime in the future as long as you have some long *pianissimo* movements in between.

But, if you choose to go loud with every series and every event, people will get smart. They'll soon learn that "loud" really means "normal." When that happens, you'll be spending a lot more time, energy, and money, but people will learn to ignore your yelling. Loud will not be loud anymore.

Before you "pull out all the stops," make sure you're really going to deliver what you promise. It better *really* be the best deal ever. If not, all that yelling will eventually lead to you losing your voice—your message will lose credibility. People will stop believing you, and they'll stop responding to your message. If everything is loud, nothing is loud.

32

Stop Trying to Be Fair

I once had lunch with a few of my teammates at a no-name restaurant. It was quite the surreal experience. Everything about the restaurant screamed 1970s—including the waitresses. One of them reprimanded me for trying to pour tea for someone else. (I'll never do that again.) Oddly enough, they were playing Madonna music over the sound system. Like I said, it was very surreal.

As we were walking out, we noticed a display of business cards. No, not just a display of individual cards, but an array of tiny trays and baskets stocked with people's cards—probably more than fifty in all—advertising varied services and vying for the attention of the restaurant patrons. You could buy a house, get your hair cut, and catch a taxi among other things. I guess we could call Sheila's Beauty Salon to see how effective this advertising is for her business since it appeared to me that she got the prime real estate on the front row.

I guess we can't fault these businesses for taking advantage of some free advertising. And, honestly, I guess we can't fault ministries in our churches for doing the same thing. At some point, though, someone in leadership probably needs to ask the question: what's the priority message?

Here's the reality, though: it's just easier to say "yes" to everyone. It's easier to treat everyone the same. Only problem is that when you try to make everyone equal and attempt to treat everyone fairly, you end up with this cluttered display of business cards.

Regrettably, this crowded shelf of business cards is reminiscent of what I see in too many churches. In an attempt to be fair, churches are willing to be less effective.

- When we promote every ministry equally, nothing gets prioritized.
- When every ministry is treated the same, it creates confusion for people trying to figure out their next step.
- When we give everyone the same platform, it's difficult for any of the messages to be heard.

The only answer to this is for leaders to be unfair. You have to determine your priorities and give those ministries the focus in your messaging. You have to be willing to say "no" to many requests for platform time and bulletin space and email blasts. You have to keep the important stuff important.

Of course, in church world, I see organizations all the time embracing the "fairness doctrine." You see it most prominently on display when it comes to communications. Every ministry, regardless of priorities, has information linked to the home page of the church's website. Every ministry, regardless of priorities, has access to announcement time and the bulletin. Every ministry, regardless of priorities, has their own logo and their own platform. We do that to be fair.

When fairness drives your communications strategy, your least important message has the same weight as your most important message. That leaves people confused and overwhelmed by all our competing messages. And, by embracing fairness, it *will* generate competition.

Businesses would never embrace the fairness doctrine. At Apple, as an example, they have hundreds of products that they're offering at any one time, but today (and every day) only one product will be featured on their home page.

We would never do that in the church, because it wouldn't be fair to the iMacs and the iPads and the iTunes and the nice people in support who are caring for all the people.

Mark Beeson, the founding and senior pastor at Granger Community Church, would frequently say, "Life is not fair, and then you die." Just because we've embraced fairness as a value in our churches doesn't mean we need to continue the tradition.

33

Insider Language

At one time I was serving part-time at West Ridge Church and part-time coaching and consulting with other churches across the country. I typically worked from my home office on Thursdays during this time, which is a critical part of the story I'm about to share.

Every Thursday I would be sitting at my desk in my home office and an email message would arrive from the church. Typically it said something simple like this: "Ralph is here in the Discovery Room." That's it. No other details.

For weeks, I got these messages, but, because I was working from home, there wasn't any way for me to investigate further on my own. Being the new guy, I didn't want to come across looking like an idiot. It was obvious that everyone else knew what this was about. It appeared that I was the only one in the dark. I was curious. Who is Ralph, and why is he in the Discovery Room?

Troy was new to the team as well. So, after several weeks of wondering what this cryptic message was all about, I finally got up the nerve to ask him. But he, like me, had not figured out who this Ralph person was. Furthermore, neither of us had any idea where the "Discovery Room" was located, which, upon further reflection, makes it a rather odd name for a room since neither of us had "discovered" it.

At least I wasn't alone at this point. I now had a cohort who shared the angst of this puzzling situation. As it turns out, Ralph is a real person. He serves in various outreach ministries at the church. And, regularly on Thursdays,

Ralph delivers leftover baked goods to the Discovery Room at the church. He shares these bakery items with the staff. It's actually quite a kind gesture.

It was a great reminder, though, that ministry can happen week after week, and, if we're not careful, the way we talk about it could leave new people in the dark. At churches I've visited, I've experienced these examples of insider language:

- Mentioning specific people by name in messages but not explaining who those people are.
- Encouraging people to go to a particular room for an event after the service, but not having any people or signs to direct people toward that room.
- Using names for ministries that have no meaning to people who don't attend the church. (We eliminated one of those at West Ridge. When we were new to the church, we had no idea that "Praiseland" was for preschoolers.)
- Telling people to talk to a specific person after the service in order to take a next step, but then not explaining who that person is or where to find them.

Generally, it's pretty easy to figure out if a church is really outside-focused based on the language it uses. This becomes particularly obvious when we start throwing out theological terms without explaining what those words mean. Take some time to gain the perspective of people who are new to the church. What great ministry might they be missing because you're holding on to insider language?

34

We Have Too Many Messages

As churches (and teachers), our intuition tells us we need new content in order to keep people engaged and help them take their next steps. I'm becoming more and more convinced, however, that we are just confusing people with every message we add. Rather than generating new content, we need to be focused on delivering the critical messages across multiple platforms.

That's why, as an example, you may have heard me address the same topic on Twitter, on my blog, in eBooks, in traditional books, and from the platform at a conference. Ben Stroup said it this way in one of his blog posts:

> The temptation for organizations is to just keep creating more and more messages while sending them across the most efficient and established models for the organization. The lie that organizations buy into is that they constantly need to have something new in order to break through the clutter and reach their target audience.

The problem, of course, is that we think we're repeating ourselves. We get bored with the same message. We assume everyone has already heard it.

The important messages need to be repeated often. They need to be shared in multiple formats. In order to do that, we need fewer messages. And we need systems to support the messages we are sharing so that people know how to take their next steps.

Remember, your message has the potential to shift thinking. Your systems have the potential to shift behaviors.

35

Platform

Michael Hyatt wrote in his book *Platform,* "Very simply, a platform is the thing you have to stand on to get heard. It's your stage. But unlike a stage in the theater, today's platform is not built of wood or concrete or perched on a grassy hill. Today's platform is built of people. Contacts. Connections. Followers." Below is a list of just some of the things I've discovered to be true when it comes to one's platform:

- There are no shortcuts to having a platform. You have to earn it.
- No one owes you a platform.
- Sometimes someone who is trusted can help you get a moment on the platform, but you still have to deliver to keep it.
- The harder you try to have a platform, the harder it is to get it.
- If you do what you're designed to do and you are faithful to stick with it over time, there's a good chance you'll have a platform.
- Not all platforms are created equal, but all have the opportunity to positively impact the lives of others.
- Relationships are the foundation of a platform. If you can't build relationships, you can't have a platform.
- The person who yells the loudest doesn't necessarily get the platform.

- If you never stop and listen, you probably won't get the platform either.
- If it's just about you, you don't have a platform.
- You'll lose your platform if you don't continue to use it for positive change. You have to move people to a better place.
- You're more likely to leverage your platform if you tell stories that engage both the head and the heart.
- You're more likely to keep your platform if you ask questions.
- If people can't have access to you and your daily life, your platform is probably shrinking, whether you know it or not.
- Platforms are established over time but lost in an instant.
- Lots of people want a platform, but very few are gifted to have a platform and even fewer are humble enough to keep it.

36

10 Ways to Generate Better Online Content

When using the Web to engage your audience, improving your content will help you engage your audience. Here are ten ways to generate better content, which have enhanced my message and ministry greatly:

1. ***Tell stories.*** The stories about *you* are the best (and see numbers 8 and 9 below).

2. ***Create compelling headlines.*** I scan headlines and only read the articles with headlines that grab my attention.

3. ***Make it scannable.*** Think bullets, lists, bold type, subheadings, pull quotes, etc.

4. ***Use pictures and video.*** Keep videos under 4 minutes whenever possible.

5. ***Become a thought leader.*** That means you need to start reading something that doesn't come from another pastor's blog. And, you need to create time to think.

6. ***Meet reader's needs.*** You have to develop relationships with your readers to figure this out.

7. **Generate a reaction or prompt an action.** Move people or frustrate people.

8. **Be vulnerable.** Share what you're learning, including the successes and the mistakes.

9. **Use humor.** Sometimes you've got to keep things light. Also, there's no better (and easier) way to be vulnerable than by showing you can laugh at yourself.

10. **Keep it brief.** I don't read long articles on the Web no matter who writes them.

Oh, and #11 would be "Start a conversation."

37

Spreading Your Message Online

A few years ago I read an article in *Fast Company* about a study completed by SocialTwist. Using widgets built into referral messages, they found that:

- *Most referrals still happen through email.* In fact, email still has more than double the referrals of social networking sites.
- *Most click-throughs happen through social networking.* Social networking accounts for almost twice as many click-throughs as email.
- *Among social networking sites, Facebook makes up more than 78 percent of the usage.* Interestingly enough, although Twitter only has five percent of the social media "market," it has a much higher click-through rate (almost six times the Facebook rate).

If you are engaged in communications at a church, what can you learn from this? Here are some strategies I think we need to consider:

1. *Online strategy involves much more than a website.* It's pointless to have a website unless you're also leveraging email and social networking strategies to point people to your site.

2. ***Email is a great tool for building an audience.*** It's still the easiest online communications tool to use; however, we need to be strategic about how we use it. There's a fine line between spamming our audience and providing a focused, helpful message. If people are going to use online communications to invite friends to church, though, they'll probably forward an email.

3. ***Social networking is a powerful tool for encouraging online engagement.*** At this point, it's not as effective for building an audience, but social networking tools, when used appropriately, will improve how your existing audience engages your online content.

4. ***You need both an email and a social networking strategy.*** Email is not going away any time soon. It's not as sexy as Facebook or Twitter, but you're missing a huge opportunity if you don't have an intentional strategy for using that communications tool.

Are these trends consistent with what you're seeing in your organizations? How is your use of these online communication tools shifting?

Now, before you get in trouble—and blame it on me—remember that I never said to neglect focusing on what you need to do and say on Sundays. So dot all your i's and cross all your t's in your preparation and give it your all this weekend, but on Monday turn your attention to your weekly message.

To help you think through all of this on a deeper level, go over the discussion questions that follow, both on your own as well as with your team. When your Monday-through-Saturday message becomes stronger, that will make your Sunday all the more richer and meaningful to those who have been attending for years as well as those who walk through your doors for the very first time.

Conclusion

I'm not a big fan of religion. It just seems to create barriers for people experiencing a vibrant relationship with Jesus. Religion values traditions. Traditions aren't necessarily a bad thing. It's when we begin to worship methods and traditions that we find ourselves in trouble. That's when the methods become more important than the message and our mission.

My main purpose for writing this book was to challenge your thinking. I want you to look hard at the church's purpose. Is the primary mission of the church being accomplished? If not, don't settle. If people aren't responding to the gospel and lives aren't being transformed, don't stick with what's predictable. Don't sell out to religion. We don't need any more safe churches filled with happy Christians. We need churches that are willing to take risks and deal with the messiness of real life. I'm tired of comfortable. I hope you are too.

I want your church to have a big impact. I'm praying you see lives changed. I'm hopeful you will have lasting influence in the communities you serve. For that to happen, though, I'm convinced it will take more than a framed vision statement hanging on the wall in your lobby.

You'll have to identify and accept why you're stuck. You'll need to embrace new strategies and systems to close the gap between your vision and the tendency to drift toward doing church the way you've always done church. You'll need to empower people to serve and lead using the gifts God has given them. You'll need to sharpen your message when the crowd is present and when you're *off* the platform.

This I know for sure—Jesus has great plans for his church. I know that because he promised, "I will build my church, and all the powers of hell will not conquer it" (Matthew 16:18). If you've gotten this far, I'm trusting you don't want your church to be stuck. Have confidence in this— God doesn't want that either. He will build his church, and he'll empower you to engage that mission. That's your purpose. Live it out.

And leave the leisure suit in the closet.

Key Ideas & Discussion Questions

Part One

The Leisure Suit Trap

Key Ideas

1. Your church may have started one hundred years ago or ten years ago or even just ten months ago—but stuck is still *stuck*.

2. We won't fully know the power and impact of the local church until people are empowered to be the people God wired them up to be.

3. A healthy vision worth pursuing must attract many more people than it turns away; however, a strong vision will always help some people determine, "That's not for me."

4. Sometimes we get stuck when internal processes are too confusing to navigate, thus stifling new ideas rather than spurring innovation.

5. Leaders have to choose between control and innovation. You can't have both.

6. Real effectiveness comes when we organize volunteers around a mission, create processes to follow up with guests and givers, and lead our staff with intentionality and intensity.

7. You can have a strong vision, but it's good systems and strategies that shift behaviors.

8. Churches stop growing when they start doing church for "insiders" instead of trying to impact the lives of people outside our walls.

Discussion Questions

1. Have you ever worn a leisure suit (or remember your father wearing one)? What did it look like? Would you wear it again if they ever came back into style?

2. What element of your ministry was once in style but is now glaringly outdated and in need of an overhaul?

3. Is your church personality-driven or vision-driven? How can you move from the former to the latter?

4. Why do you agree or disagree that a clearly defined vision actually allows for more freedom?

5. In what ways are you empowering people so they can impact your church and its ministry? If you're not doing so, how can you empower them?

6. Why do you agree or disagree with the description of the four different stages of leadership growth (Lead by Example, Lead Other People, Lead Other Leaders, and Lead by Vision)? Where is your church? Is it where it needs to be?

7. What do you need to do today to prepare to step into a new leadership role tomorrow?

8. When you suffered defeat in the past (or at least did not experience success), how did you respond with victim-thinking or avoid doing so?

9. Considering your organizational structure and internal processes, how have they changed over the past three to five years? If they are the same, why is that?

10. What are the dangers of implementing permanent solutions to temporary problems? When have you done so, and how can you avoid doing so in the future?

11. Is the structure of your church simple or complex? How is that working out for you? Are you fleet of foot or too bogged down to move?

12. Is your church more like a 30-year-old sedan or a late-model sports car? What past successes are you still basking in when you should be looking to future victories?

13. Chick-fil-A founder Truett Cathy once said "When we get better the customer will force us to get bigger." How do the activities of your church contribute to, or support, your core values and mission? Where do you need to get "better" before doing anything else?

14. What are your core values and mission? How can you make sure everyone on your staff and in your congregation know what they are?

15. Do you know what percentage of your congregation is volunteering? How can you grow that number?

16. What ministry roles and responsibilities currently on a staff member's plate (even yours!) need to be handed over to volunteers?

17. Would an outsider say that your church is full of happy Christians or hurting, lost people who need Jesus? What practical steps can you take to move your focus to the "outsiders"?

Part Two

Hanging Up the Leisure Suit

Key Ideas

1. Many churches—and, in fact, many denominations—would rather stay stuck and eventually die rather than make changes that might make people (including leaders) feel uncomfortable.

2. It's possible for everyone to know the vision but still not have any clue what they're supposed to do to help make the vision become reality.

3. Where God provides a vision, he also seems to provide a system or strategy to accomplish that vision.

4. The *purpose* has to be the priority—if that's not the case, the organization can become unbalanced and grow unhealthy.

5. If your systems are broken or lacking, you can teach all you want . . . but it's not going to change behaviors.

6. Good people using bad systems will never produce good results. Normal people using good systems can produce great results.

Discussion Questions

1. Just as leisure suits are no longer fashionable, what about your church is out of style? (Think back to the first part of this book.)

2. What companies, sports teams, or other organizations seem to be stuck right now? What are the main reasons for them being in their predicament?

3. What strategies, rules, or activities have you been doing for a while now without success? Why do you keep doing the same thing over and over hoping for different results?

4. Look at the list of symptoms prevalent in churches that are stuck. Which of these could be used to describe your church? What should be on that list based on your experience?

5. Consider this quote from Jim Collins: "Those in power blame other people or external factors—or otherwise explain away the data—rather than confront the frightening reality that the enterprise may be in serious trouble." What excuses have you or others in your church been making in order to avoid facing what may be a "frightening realty"?

6. Without cheating, recite—or at least summarize— from heart your church's vision statement, if you can. How many people in your congregation know it?

7. Supposing you and most people in your church know the vision statement, do people know how to turn it into reality? Why or why not?

8. On a scale of 1 to 10 (with 1 being a crack in the sidewalk and 10 being the Grand Canyon), how wide is the gap between vision and the people who are waiting to execute that vision?

9. Consider the warning signs that your ministry may not be "minding the gap." Which ones are true about your church? Are there any more that should be added to this list?

10. As I've pointed out, there are a number of examples of God using systems to accomplish his purpose. Which one speaks to you most profoundly? How do these biblical accounts relate to how your church operates?

11. With all this talk about systems and strategies, and the gap between vision and reality, where do you feel God fits in?

12. When God wants to accomplish something through us, he often provides a specific strategy for getting it done. When have you noticed that to be true in the past? What vision do you have right now for which you're still waiting on a divine strategy?

13. Before reading this document, why would you have described your church as either healthy or unhealthy?

14. Read through the six elements of a healthy organization again. In your church, which areas are in need of a serious overhaul? Where are you stuck most of all?

15. *Purpose* has to be the priority, otherwise a church will become unbalanced and unhealthy. What

areas in your ministry are getting too much attention, and which ones are being neglected?

16. How many different opportunities/settings are in your church where people are taught? (Consider adults, students, children, and other specific groups.)

17. Which of these teaching opportunities end with knowledge only, and which ones lead people to move forward in action?

18. A healthy system is a simple, replicable process to help people move from where they are to where God wants them to be. How would you describe the current state of your system?

19. Knowing that your church is unique, what common characteristics do you believe are the most important in a healthy system?

20. Consider this quote from Scott Belsky: "The more people who lie awake in bed thinking about your idea, the better. But people only obsess about ideas when they feel a sense of ownership." In what ways have you made sure that those around you feel complete ownership and are free to make decisions within established boundaries?

21. What are the key touch points in your church? What systems do you have in place (or need to establish) so that people are able to take the next step necessary?

22. Where have you seen good people using bad systems? Where have you witnessed "normal" people using systems to create great results?

23. Now that you've taken the first step toward getting unstuck by going through these questions and taking a long, hard look at your ministry, what is the first thing you need to do tomorrow?

Part Three

Stayin' Alive

Key Ideas

1. One generation of ministry doesn't make a legacy—you need to prepare the next generation for continued impact.

2. If you are trying to be a manager when you're actually a leader, you will be unfulfilled and face ministry burnout. If you're forced into a leadership role when you're actually a manager, you will face the same challenges.

3. We may *say* that we trust God to lead us where he wants us to go and to do what he wants us to do, but when we micromanage, we communicate something quite different.

4. What consensus is for the most part—almost all the time—is an attempt to overly manage outcome, which unfortunately holds you back from going to where God wants you to move.

5. It's possible to do the work of God without doing the work God has called you to do.

6. Empowering other leaders to build healthier organizations may get messy along the way, but you will end up in a place where your organization

can have a much bigger impact and more people will be fulfilled in their roles.

7. For the ministry of the local church to remain effective, you need to be a leader who is comfortable with being uncomfortable.

Discussion Questions

1. In what ways are you "stayin' alive" as a leader—not just existing but thriving?

2. What path do you have in place to help young, gifted leaders grow and gain responsibility and authority?

3. If leadership is no longer a title on a business card, what is it? How have you seen it played out around you?

4. So, what are *you* doing to prepare the next generation for continued impact?

5. Are you a leader or a manager? Are those around you leaders or managers?

6. Whether you and those around you are leaders or managers, how are you fulfilling your roles according to your gifts?

7. How close are you to experiencing ministry burnout? How do you ensure that you keep doing what God created you to do?

8. How would you have responded had you been Joshua about to lead the Israelites through the Jordan River? Not knowing the outcome? Not fully in control?

9. What's your unspoken motto as a leader: "If I don't do it, no one will" or "If I do it, no one will do it"? Why? What necessary steps do you need to take in order to be less of a control freak?

10. Why do you agree or disagree that "consensus sucks"? In what situations have you witnessed consensus being a help or a hindrance in your ministry?

11. Why is it "better to fix problems than to prevent them," as Pixar president Ed Catmull says? What opportunities have you missed out on because you overplanned and missed the mark?

12. In what ways have you ever caught yourself doing the work of God without doing the work God has called you to do? What is the difference?

13. What changes do you need to make in your own leadership style that allows you to do what you need to do and others to do what they need to do?

14. Are you a "Complete the Right Task" or "Hire the Right People" type of leader? What's the difference you've seen in your ministry?

15. Would you add anything else to the list of differences between delegation and empowerment? In what ways can you empower other leaders around you?

16. What challenges have you faced in leading creatives?

17. After looking over the list of tips for leading creatives, what changes do you need to make with specific people on your staff? How do you think

they'll respond to you leading them in a different way?

18. When have you ever tried to fix your boss? And is anyone on your staff trying to fix you right now?

19. How comfortable are you at being *uncomfortable*?

20. How can you force yourself into some less-comfortable situations in order to grow as a leader?

Part Four

Get Your Groove On

Key Ideas

1. Like it or not, the message you send out during the week—good or bad, spoken or unspoken—is marketing at its core.

2. You cannot force people to think about what they need until they know they need it, so get to know individuals, families, and their needs.

3. It's not the name. It's the quality of the product or service or the experience that matters.

4. If you don't address the more challenging questions at hand, good marketing will just help an unhealthy organization fail faster.

5. Loud is only effective when it's louder than normal. If it's always loud, then loud becomes the new normal.

6. When fairness drives your communications strategy, your least important message has the same weight as your most important message, which leaves people confused.

7. It's pretty easy to figure out if a church is really outside-focused based on the language it uses.

8. Rather than generating new content, we need to be focused on delivering the critical messages across multiple platforms.

Discussion Questions

1. Before reading this book, would you have claimed to be a proponent of church marketing? Why or why not?

2. What types of marketing have you been doing without realizing it?

3. What are you doing to make your church marketing more effective? What is currently working or not working well for you?

4. In the list of "10 Ways to Improve Marketing Without Spending Any Money," which two or three tips stood out to you most?

5. Which of these "10 Ways" strategies have you used in the past or are currently employing? What was the outcome? What would you add to this list?

6. If the name doesn't matter until the brand is established, how can you spend more time improving your brand?

7. When have you jumped to marketing tactics too quickly? When has marketing worked but probably not been the right thing to do?

8. Look back at the nine questions in the "Why Churches Should Stop Marketing" chapter. What marketing do you need to stop immediately?

9. Are you LOUD all the time in your marketing efforts? How can you vary the dynamics of your message so that you build crescendo that people will actually hear and respond to?

10. What are your thoughts on fairness in promoting ministries within your church? When have your efforts to be fair resulted in hurting or weakening a ministry that is core to your mission as a church?

11. What messages are you sending out that sound like a foreign language to many in your congregation? Maybe you should sit down with a focus group of newcomers to find out what you need to clarify or change altogether.

12. What great ministry might they be missing because you're holding on to insider language?

13. What important messages need to be repeated often? And which ones need to be put aside to make room for the more important ones?

14. Do you have a platform? If not, how can you build one? If so, what are you doing to keep it?

15. Looking at the list of ten ways to generate better online content, where are you the strongest and where are you the weakest? What would you add to the list?

16. What forms of social media are working best for you individually and also for the church in general? In what areas do you need more help?

About the Author

Tony Morgan is the Chief Strategic Officer and founder of TonyMorganLive.com. He's a consultant, leadership coach, and writer who helps churches get unstuck and have a bigger impact. More important, he has a passion for people. He's all about helping people meet Jesus and take steps in their faith.

For fourteen years, Tony served on the senior leadership teams at West Ridge Church (Dallas, GA), NewSpring Church (Anderson, SC), and Granger Community Church (Granger, IN). With Tim Stevens, Tony has co-authored *Simply Strategic Stuff*, *Simply Strategic Volunteers*, and *Simply Strategic Growth*—each of which offers valuable, practical solutions for different aspects of church ministry. His book *Killing Cockroaches* (B&H Publishing) challenges leaders to focus on the priorities in life and ministry. His most recent books on leadership and ministry strategy are available on Kindle.

Tony has also written several articles on staffing, technology, strategic planning, and leadership published by organizations like *Outreach Magazine*, Catalyst, and Pastors.com. Tony and his wife, Emily, live near Atlanta, Georgia, with their four children—Kayla, Jacob, Abby, and Brooke.

For more information:
www.TonyMorganLive.com

Follow Tony on Twitter:
@TonyMorganLive

Church Consulting & Coaching

Tony Morgan loves consulting with, speaking to, and coaching leaders. Based on his experiences working for three growing churches and many church clients, he helps churches get unstuck and have a bigger impact. Let him help you with:

- **Ministry Health Assessment**—Complete a comprehensive assessment of your ministry and identify strategic next steps.
- **Strategic Operating Plan**—Clarify your mission, vision, and core strategies—and then create the right structure and accountability to realize it through prioritized action initiatives.
- **Staffing & Structure Review**—Determine the best organizational structure for future growth and get the right people in the right roles.
- **Leadership Coaching Networks**—Participate with no more than twelve people in a mentoring process to help you take your next steps as a leader.

Additionally, he partners with some great organizations to assist churches with creative design, technology, multisite, executive recruiting, stewardship, facility design and construction, and brand strategy.

Discover how Tony can partner with you:
http://tonymorganlive.com/services/